# From My Poems To Yours

## (The Live Versions)

## BRIAN DORN

# SHIRES PRESS

4869 Main Street
P.O. Box 2200
Manchester Center, VT 05255
www.northshire.com

## From My Poems To Yours
### (The Live Versions)

Copyright © 2015 Brian Dorn

ISBN Number: 978-1-60571-270-3

*Building Community, One Book at a Time*
*A family-owned, independent bookstore in*
*Manchester Ctr., VT, since 1976 and Saratoga Springs, NY since 2013.*
*We are committed to excellence in bookselling.*
*The Northshire Bookstore's mission is to serve as a resource for*
*information, ideas, and entertainment while honoring the needs of*
*customers, staff, and community.*

*Printed in the United States of America*

# CONTENTS  (In Alphabetical Order)

## BACK IN THE DAY

Just a hundred years ago
There wasn't even radio
No Nintendo or cell phones
Nothing Jetson, just Flintstones

No television or play stations
Only books and an imagination
No e-mail or computers
Nor, highways or parking meters

Air travel had yet to take off
Death was common from a cough
Photography was all the rage
No dinners from the microwave

No malls or super centers
Only shops and tonic vendors
Yet, politicians still started wars
And, even then, guns beat swords

Technology has come a long way
Not as simple as back in the day
Two world wars and nuclear fission
Man's entitled to a few bad decisions

Brian Dorn

## WORDS

Numbers aren't my thing
They are symbolically shallow
They attach themselves to strings
And they fluctuate in value

I'd rather immerse myself in letters
Erecting words for pleasure
The more meaningful, the better
Their true worth cannot be measured

There are words to live by
And words to sample
Words as diverse
As they are ample

Some words are divisive
And others are friendly
Many are durable
While others are trendy

Each are purposeful
In many different ways
Words we depend on
And words meant for play

You say I've got a way with words
Unlike those you've ever heard
Feeling it in lieu of music
Confessing you've connected to it

Captivated by what I say
Every emotion I've parlayed
Indulging in my intriguing art
Dissecting every intricate part

Imagine if we could switch places
Swap identities and exchange faces

You'd be me and I'd be you
Spending the day in each other's shoes

Thinking your thoughts as you thought mine
You'd know my poetry line-for-line

I'd get to know you inside and out
And you'd get what every word is about

Brian Dorn

## MY IMPROPRIETY

Makes me wonder what to say
As your feelings turn away
Leaving my face hanging

Makes me wonder what to think
How it changes in a blink
In water falling from your eyes

Makes me wonder what to do
Here alone, without you
Dangled by these puppet strings

I sought to live a part of you
And gave to bind us one from two
I find it all to fade away
To live is losing one more day

But life goes on
Or, so they say
Though barely functioning
And disengaged

Each day passing
In the same hard way
Full of unforeseen circumstances
And unexpected delays

I'm sorry for what I've done
I'm sorry for who I've been
Sorry for where it's gone
So sorry to lose a friend

I'm sorry I let you down
I'm sorry things can't be the same
Sorry for my impropriety
So sorry I'm the one to blame

I'm sorry I wasn't strong enough
I'm sorry for not following through
Sorry for dropping the ball
So sorry for me and you

What would it take to fix my mistake
And start all over again
Just ask me to change, act a little less strange
And all will return to normal
Or, turn me around, not say a sound
And pretend it didn't happen

Brian Dorn

## OUT OF WHACK

From communists in Vietnam
To terrorists in Afghanistan
The fighting never seems to end
There's always something to defend

We fight and fight and fight some more
Fighting Al-Qaeda to even the score
Finding any reason for the next battle
Undeterred by the lines we straddle

All I want is peace and tranquility
A world polite with simple civility

To offer respect and expect the same
Some common courtesy and sincere shame

A world without any trespassing signs
Every border wide open all of the time

Fighting wars just like before
Hate to think how many more
Hour by hour dying for power
Digging graves and laying flowers
Killing men again and again
That's the way it's always been

Our sense of priority is out of whack
Why not adjust our plan of attack
Shift our battle to the war on poverty
Quit treating it like some trite novelty
Make feeding the poor our primary business
And put our money where their mouth is

Brian Dorn

## THREE DAYS

Pentecostal, Methodist, Baptist
Presbyterian, Lutheran, and Catholic
Some traditional, others charismatic
All worshipping the same fanatic

Came not for the righteous but for sinners
From a few fish served five thousand dinners
Cured the crippled and resurrected the dead
Fulfilled every sign the prophets had said

Coerced plain water into wine
Granted forgiveness of our crimes
Came not to rule, but to serve
A Lord more gracious than we deserve

Taught His principles to the twelve
Love your neighbors as yourselves
With a kiss, He'd be betrayed
Within a tomb, His body laid

In three days, He had risen
Appeared to Mary like a vision
Removed all doubt from Thomas' head
Placed his fingers where He'd bled

Brian Dorn

## PLAIN TO SEE

She is simply beautiful
That is plain to see
Maybe not a temptress
But lovely in her subtlety

She is simply stunning
That is plain to see
Maybe not a knockout
But lovely in her subtlety

She is simply picturesque
That is plain to see
Maybe not a centerfold
But lovely in her subtlety

She is simply striking
That is plain to see
Maybe not a bombshell
But lovely in her subtlety

She is simply alluring
That is plain to see
Maybe not a covergirl
But lovely in her subtlety

Brian Dorn

## NO COMMENT

"No comment" is NOT a valid answer
It happens to be a cop out
It doesn't resolve a thing
It only multiplies the doubt

"No comment" never does suffice
In matters of concern
Coupled words cloaked in mystery
Unable to be adequately discerned

"No comment" makes a statement
If you are able to interpret its meaning
Exactly what "no comment" spells out
Depends which way the letters are leaning

"No comment" muddles the discussion
Averting exchanges of give and take
Coyly evading the conversation
Making no effort to elaborate

"No comment" could mean almost anything
Its intent is to hinder the truth
It's a way of delaying the inevitable
But there's no way of preventing its use

Brian Dorn

## BROKEN

She's stunning by nature
Cunning by nurture
Remarkably structured
Emotionally sutured

She's tragically scripted
Though flawlessly sculptured
Publicly featured
But privately tortured

Her smile is forced
She's suffering remorse
Her pain is clearly apparent

She's in obvious mourning
In need of reassuring
Her hopes have all been shattered

Words barely spoken
Her heart clearly broken
Her spirit demoralized

Who is she, what's her story
From her eyes, she's casting worry
They can't relate to how she feels
But, by my pain, our bond is sealed

Brian Dorn

## LUCK

I've been unlucky in life
My numbers never come up
And in matters of love
I'm never lucky enough

Luck is seldom on my side
More often it's my nemesis
Regardless of what I try
Luck tends to cause me fits

Good luck is never around
While bad luck tends to follow me
Luck has a way of letting me down
Almost as if we were family

If I could buy myself luck
I'd purchase all I could devour
If I couldn't afford that much
I'd rent luck by the hour

If I could get lucky with you
I'd pay anything for that
If that were to come true
I'd pray my luck would last

Brian Dorn

## CLEAR INTO SPACE

You launch me clear into space
With the flash of your eyes
You light up my face
With your playful replies

You've got me floating on air
With your indelible impression
With attraction to spare
You've revived my expression

I enjoy your vernal fragrance
And your seasonal hair
Your impractical sense
And your flavorful flare

I adore the way that you laugh
And your zest for adventure
Your sensitive half
Even the half that I've censored

I love how you do as you dare
Always pressing your luck
Acting like you don't care
But really caring too much

Brian Dorn

## RESISTING CLOSURE

My desire is still burning
Thoughts of you keep returning
But I'm afraid you never will

I've been trying to explain
How I've accepted the blame
But you don't even seem to care

I'm drowning in the blues
Inundated by the truth
But unable to accept it

Abandoned and busted
Discarded and rusted
I'm in urgent need of repair

The angst inside of me
Is in need of a remedy
Some tender loving care

Aspirin won't do
I don't have the flu
I'd be cured if you were here

Stubbornly resisting closure
Broadening my exposure
Pursuing a reconciliation

Strategically taking action
Waiting for a reaction
Hoping for a change of heart

Refusing to abort
Even as a last resort
Unwilling to let you go

Brian Dorn

## IF YOU KNEW

So confused, myself to find
Who's in you that makes me blind
Lost in love, bound to solitude
Would you find me if you knew

What's it worth to see me cry
If truth hurts, imagine lies
Hide away from faith I lack
Into her I cower back

How much could you really know
How clearly do I let it show
Does it ever make you wonder
What I'm feeling deep down under

Eyes that only dance with yours
Deep inside a love endures
Ballads sung through quivered smiles
Serenades my soul a while

To think of you each day more
I've never burned in this before
Try to leave, but long to stay
Hold you in, or cast away

Brian Dorn

## ANYTHING AND EVERYTHING

I can pardon you
If you can pardon me
Of anything and everything
But you're reluctant to agree

What kind of word is absurd
Is that really what you think of me
Don't believe everything you've heard
Nor, everything you think you see

I know it makes no sense to you
Just give me a moment to explain
You're assuming that it's all true
Don't leave me pleading here in vain

Rafting in your current
Emotions raging strong
Torn by jagged rocks
As rapids drag me down

Clinging to the hope
A calm will come along
Drowning in your tears
As doubts spin all around

Brian Dorn

## DO AS WE SAY

You can't have them
It wouldn't be fair
They're ours to deter
Don't even dare

Just sell us your oil
Everything will be fine
Don't think about nukes
That wouldn't be kind

Don't do as we do
Do as we say
We had them first
We can blow you away

If you think we're bluffing
It's time that you knew
They're locked and loaded
And aiming at you

Proclaiming words of disobedience
Blatantly inciting mass-malfeasance
Remarking on the state of society
That's the politics of poetry

Weapons of mass destruction
Lie hidden under ground
Like government corruption
Waiting to be found

Leaping to conclusions
The debacle of the century
Just an optical illusion
Merely mistaken identity

Hoodwinked, bamboozled
And bumbling the case
Duped and made fools of
Apple pie in the face

Making statements in the form of art
Millions of poets playing their part
Recording injustice and calling attention
Shouting out for intervention

Proclaiming words of disobedience
Blatantly inciting mass-malfeasance
Remarking on the state of society
That's the politics of poetry

Brian Dorn

## HIGH WIRE

You are my lesson in love
My perpetual mistake
My Pandora's box
My colossal earthquake

You jumble my senses
And dismantle my formations
Annihilate my defenses
And crumble my foundations

You're my oceanic swim
My volcanic eruption
My atmospheric spin
My erroneous assumption

You dominate my thoughts
And coax my attention
You perpetuate my faults
Superseding all prevention

You're my terminal affliction
My forbidden desire
My choice of addiction
My perilous high wire

Brian Dorn

## PROPHECY

Left alone and petrified
All my actions magnified
Wallowing in what I've done

All this pain, it permeates
As her feelings dissipate
Cursed by my ineptitude

Crushed in my assertion
Spent by vain exertion
Frozen in my own self-doubt

My prophecy fulfilled
Foolish to be willed
Never can it be undone

Seeking solace in soulful hymns
Praying forgiveness of my whims
Yet stapled to my condemnation

Crashing into guarded gates
Fading into altered states
Sulking in my own self-pity

Brian Dorn

## LESSONS

Child's play isn't what it used to be
Our kids are on a vengeance spree
Violence is a crying shame
Why not learn to play peace games
Why not learn to play peace games

That's the price we've paid
The debt we owe
The bed we've made
The heirloom we've sold

That's the fix we're in
The flames we fanned
Our shallow win
And the schemes we've planned

That's the seeds we've sowed
And the bridges burned
The fibs we've told
And our lessons learned
And our lessons learned

Everything we thought was right
And struggled for with all our might

Everything we've ever known
And all the lessons life has shown

For all the times to be forgiven
Of all the errors we've been living

With everything that's come and gone
Still, it seems, we end up wrong
Still, it seems, we end up wrong

Brian Dorn

## ELUSIVE WORDS

Pursuing a poignant perspective
Filtering out the imperfections
Trying to develop a marketable product
Something verbally melodic

What's that word
Why won't it come to me
That elusive word
Deep down inside of me

Combing my thought-ways
For the fugitive in mind
The manhunt is underway
To apprehend him this time

Creating my own mark of expression
Hoping to leave a lasting impression
Aiming to make it truly compelling
Writing something worthy of selling

Free verse
For what it's worth
Is no bargain at all

Packaged rhyme-free
But sweetened
To please

It remains
Priced the same
As pure poetry

There is plenty to be said
In what poetry proposes
But a poem without rhyme
Is but a bouquet without roses

Pursuing a poignant perspective
Filtering out the imperfections
Trying to develop a marketable product
Something verbally melodic

Creating my own mark of expression
Hoping to leave a lasting impression
Aiming to make it truly compelling
Writing something worthy of selling

Brian Dorn

## ENVY'S CARNAGE

The damage has been done
Things may never be the same
As much as I wish otherwise
Your heart remains estranged

So rash of you to reach this verdict
Why not accept me as imperfect
Before to know me as your hero
Now to judge me less than zero

The damage has been done
Things may never be the same
As much as I wish otherwise
Your heart remains estranged

Taking rounds of friendly fire
Shot to hell by my desire
Victim of collateral damage
All caught up in envy's carnage

The damage has been done
Things may never be the same
As much as I wish otherwise
Your heart remains estranged

What else could I expect
I knew exactly how you'd react
Considering the circumstance
How could we remain intact

I'm throwing in the towel
This time it's for sure
Battered by the past
I can't fight it anymore

We will go on living
Leading separate lives
Independent of each other
As I dubiously get by

It would take a miracle
To eliminate your doubt
Something supernatural
Only fate could figure out

Brian Dorn

## HARD AS STONE

How it must feel
To be built out of steel
With titanium bones
And a heart hard as stone

How healthy you'd feel
Having no wounds to heal
No feelings to spare
Or, any reason to care

How free you would feel
With no secrets to veil
No crosses to bare
Or a conscience to clear

How safe it would feel
To have nothing to steal
Just to live as you choose
With no face to lose

Unwilling to bend
Standing firm till the end
With no emotions visible
So seemingly invincible

I wish I could be that way
Even if for just one day
Feeling like I've got it made
If only I could be that way

Sometimes, it's easier not to care
Taking chances as you dare
Doesn't matter who gets hurt
Or, to what revenge they might resort

Just to do it your own way
Unconcerned with what they'd say
Living life one whim at a time
How is that some sort of crime

Brian Dorn

## DIVINE THOUGHT

I'm a product of our society
Forced-fed its ideology
What I learned is what they taught
Influenced by what they thought

Naively fooled by the public school
Where divinity has been overruled
Taught to doubt my own intuition
And made to worship man's fruition

Absorbing what they had to say
Methodically programmed along the way
Molding my impressionable mind
Blindly following the blind

The things that I've always known
Are the very things I know bemoan
I should have questioned it long before
As more hard facts became unsure

Told exactly what to learn
Scripture was of no concern
His fundamentals had been storaged
Divine thought profanely discouraged

Brian Dorn

## SUSPENDED IN TIME

Four eyes suspended in time
Two of yours and two of mine
Winter brown and summer green
Mingling in an optic stream

It's a small world
Built just for two
Everything revolving
Around me and you

The clouds are mine
And the moon is yours
You've got the oceans
And I'll take the shore

I'll surf on your waves
And you'll explore my dry land
I'll splash in your puddles
And you'll play in my sand

We'll float on my clouds
And admire your moon
Bask in the silence
And relish its tune

Brian Dorn

## MAKE IT RIGHT

It's time to forgive and let live
Just let bygones be

We're less different than we are alike
Why in the world do we continue to fight
Why is it so difficult to find common ground
We're all riding on the same merry-go-round

It's time to forgive and let live
Just let bygones be

Passively leading a civil war
A movement worthy of dying for

His message transcending time and space
Inspiring the whole human race

Great are the words of MLK
We're thankful that he had his say

Instrumental in the progress we've seen
Moving us closer to realizing his dream

It's time to forgive and let live
Just let bygones be
Quit taking sides, swallow your pride
Let it go and set it free
Give up the fight, make it right
And embrace diversity

It's time to forgive and let live
Just let bygones be

Don't be so greedy
Be generous instead
Nourish the hungry
Revive what's dead

Be neighbor friendly
Make prudent decisions
Protect our environment
Reduce harmful emissions

Exalt the humble
And oppose the proud
Push for equality
For crying out loud

Promote global peace
Respect each other
Donate your talents
Assist one another

Lead by example
Demonstrate class
End the prejudice
Don't live in the past

Brian Dorn

## TRYING SMILE

How do we find happiness
Could we find it in a kiss
Your mouth pressed up to mine
Might it make it all feel fine
For, only you are in my heart
So sad we are a world apart

Nestled by hope and passionate desire
Isle of love encircled by fire
Colors of dreams mixed yellow and blue
Hours envisioned souly of you
Oceans of thoughts drift deeper each day
Lost to the past as fate finds her way

Right side up switched outside in
Overboard and in tailspin
Spun around, turned upside down
Fighting duels in jaded towns

Dishing dirt and slinging mud
Talking trash and holding a grudge
Accusations go round and round
Tossing us in lost and found

From brown eyes, I wipe a tear
In my thoughts, I find you near
Left in me a trying smile
Like a fad gone out of style

Difficult to let it go
Harder than you'd ever know
In my love, I'd wish to try
And in my mind I reason why

Brian Dorn

## GIVE IT A TRY

We all have a talent
Each endowed with a skill
Some more or less gallant
But all meant to thrill
Find your purpose
Your reason for being
Allow it to surface
Seeing is believing

Do yourself a favor
Allow passions to spark
Seek moments to savor
And journeys to embark

There are roads left to travel
And unopened gates
More scrolls to unravel
In discovering your fate
You've got plenty to say
Bold statements to make
Avoid further delay
Your destiny is at stake

It's time you believe in your passion
And your creativity
It's time you believe in your voice
And your personality

It's time you believe in your strength
And your resiliency
It's time you believe in your purpose
And your ingenuity
It's time you believe in your self-worth
And your validity
It's time you believe in your future
And act accordingly

Focused on my destination
Avoiding further hesitation
I've got a challenge to mount
Determined to make it work
Embracing my eccentric quirks
Making my best effort count
Refusing to let life pass me by
Resolving to give it a try
Considering what might amount

The coast is clear
And the sailing is smooth
My destination is near
And I'm on the move
I've got the wind at my back
And I've lessened my load
Leaving behind my past
My fate behold

Brian Dorn

## AMBUSHED

So, I find you gave me up
His side you've taken all along
Your message never more abrupt
How it hurts to be so wrong

Ambushed by the two of you
Like some calculated ploy
Nice to know who you're loyal to
Sworn vows deemed null and void

Things I've always tried to hide
In confidence, I've told you all
I find you've tossed my cross aside
From this trust, so hard I fall

You've got me figured out
That's what you do
And I'm in the red
On account of you

You've audited my books
That much is true
And I'm deep in debt
On account of you

You've crunched my numbers
And earned your due
And I'm destitute
On account of you

I can't believe you sold me out
Publicizing what I'm all about
Shattering my frail serenity
Cruelly exposing my true identity

Brian Dorn

## CAN'T ESCAPE

From the corner of my eye
Hard to fathom what I saw
Turned my head as if to try
And into love so deep I fall

Unlike I've ever felt before
It tossed and turned me like a storm
Nothing's made me troubled more
Nor, ever have I felt so warm

Eyes that capture mine in chains
Oh, so tightly locked to yours
Finding comfort in this pain
Gripped so tight forever more

Don't ever let me look away
Please never, never let me go
In your eyes I want to stay
In your heart I want to grow

So content you make me feel
Alive inside your garden eyes
Nothing's ever felt so real
Can't escape, won't even try

Brian Dorn

## FROM MY POEMS TO YOURS

Uniquely different, you and I
But, doing as we damn well please
We're products of intelligent design
No settling for mediocrity

Poetically inclined and wired to rhyme
Economy of word our specialty
United in our same frame of mind
On an airline of creativity

Brazen, bold, and expression stone cold
Unabashed and self-promoted
Sifting through thoughts for solid gold
My love poems served sugarcoated

Unshrouded, outed and oxidized
Stripped of guilt and irrational fear
Unapologetic and diversified
Kings of our own atmosphere

Nothing off-limits, every word fair play
From arousal to anticlimactic
Pesky emotions caught in the fray
Some subtle, others clearly emphatic

Brian Dorn

## ROUND AND ROUND

Where do we go from here
What's left for us to do
Sometimes it seems the end is near
Why doesn't it feel like it used to

Where's our hopes and aspiration
Seems that life has dragged us down
Struggling each day in exasperation
Every smile turned to frowns

Our songs no longer sound the same
Records spinning round and round
Losing track of the game
No more passion to be found

Time just seems to drag on by
If only it could go by faster
Our well of love has run dry
Same old routine, same old master

Imagine to be free again
Free of suspicion, free of disdain
Fully pardoned of my sentence
Freedom from this ball and chain

Free to go where I want to go
No one there to block my way
Free to know who I want to know
No warden locking me away

I've put your needs ahead of mine
In spite of my own happiness
But, it seems, it's finally time
To be released from this stress

I feel it's in your best interest
Actually, it's best for both of us
You say my actions are so careless
It's just like you to make a fuss

Brian Dorn

## REALITY CHECK

It all goes south from here
Decomposing into nowhere
Every moment sinking lower
My reactions so much slower
Feeling totally forgotten
Like an apple that's gone rotten

Cynical and in no particular hurry
Doubting every single story
Every day the heart beats colder
That's the state of growing older

Mired in compounding strife
Devoid of purpose in this life
Given up on fruitless dreams
Nothing ever as it seemed

Unwilling to stand and fight
Depleted every ounce of might
Conditioned to expect the worst
Optimism has run its course

In pursuit of validation
Nursing emotional lacerations
Disillusioned and disenchanted
Every opinion has been slanted

Singled out and double-crossed
Losing faith and getting lost
On my own and feeling slighted
Unacknowledged and blind-sided

Facing a reality check
Feeling like a train wreck
Bogged down in trepidation
Leery of likely retaliation

Losing trust in modern man
Nothing going as I planned
In disarray and failure bound
Destined to be let down

Brian Dorn

## WE ALL

We all struggle - We all hope
We all suffer - We all cope
We all rejoice - We all ache
We all give - We all take

We all smile - We all frown
We all gloat - We all mourn
We all laugh - We all cry
We all live - We all die

We all try - We all stumble
We all score - We all fumble
We all lose - We all win
We all abide - We all sin

We all sacrifice - We all desire
We all settle - We all aspire
We all believe - We all doubt
We all joke - We all pout

We all fight - We all bruise
We all shun - We all choose
We all dream - We all shatter
We all exist - therefore We matter

Brian Dorn

## MONKEY BARS

What's the deal with evolution
Man's scientific revolution
Just a theory or proven fact
Educated guess or more exact

They say that it's a monkey thing
Homo Sapiens from ding-a-ling
Changing shape and intellect
In our quest to stand erect

If we've evolved, why not them
Our relatives need join the trend
Still swinging on their monkey bars
We've moved on to driving cars

Don't believe as Darwin does
His fabled concept never was
Another goof by fallible man
Fooling with the Master plan

We painstakingly dig up the past
As our cousins scratch their ass
Waiting impatiently to evolve
Going ape as their hopes dissolve

Brian Dorn

## CREATIVE SIDE

Viewing old photos of me as a boy
Playing with my favorite toys
Who would I grow up to be
Never imagined someone like me

Differentiating possession from plural
No interest in the corporate world
Disregarding investment opportunities
Seeking shelter in common poetry

Common bonds and common beliefs
Common behavior and common grief
Common experience and common emotions
Common failures and common notions
Common feelings and common goals
Common people and common souls
Common concerns and common expressions
Trying to make an uncommon impression

Laying it all on the line
Line after line after line
Sharing with you what is mine
Time after time after time

My virtues and my flaws
My personal thoughts and reflections
Life's inevitable seesaws
My private introspection

Both factual and fiction
Much of which lies in between
My numerous contradictions
Shrouded secrets being seen

Bringing poetry to life
None of which is perfect
My issues brought to light
My conscience having surfaced

Every line that's been written
Reviewed and scrutinized
My convenient omissions
And my psyche analyzed

The solution is in my hand
And I'm writing it all out
Scripting my impending plans
No longer mired in self-doubt

I'm swallowing my pride
Making up for lost time
Nurturing my creative side
And broadening my mind

Brian Dorn

## THE LOVE POEM

Love is understanding
Love is compromise
Love is generosity
Love is sacrifice

Love does not discriminate
Love is free of charge
Love is the solution
Love is who we are

Love is universal
Love is Heaven-sent
Love was fastened to the cross
Love's greatest testament

Love is triumphant
Love is somersaults
Love is compassion
Love is free of fault

Love is forgiveness
Love offers a hand
Love is eternal
Love is His command

Brian Dorn

## CHEMICAL SMILE

Just can't describe how it makes me feel
So incomparable, hardly seems real
Nothing's ever touched me this way
How just your smile can lighten my day

So much more than how your mouth moves
Way beyond the way your lips groove
Maybe it's in those mushroom eyes
Or wrapped inside some brilliant disguise

It pours over me like a waterfall
Washing my troubles, flooding over my walls
However I'm feeling, it alters my mood
All of my worries somehow removed

Just one more fix before you go
I need it so much more than you know
It takes over me and holds for a while
Just one more dose of your chemical smile

Brian Dorn

## GHOST TOWN

Reminding me how wrong it went
What these places really meant
Finding you in where I go
Faces seen through falling snow

Stranded in a ghost-town haze
Feelings that don't go away
In themes of movies I attend
Reliving pain that doesn't end

Songs played on the radio
Scents of you, to me they blow
Wrongs that left me lonely here
Laments in me a somber tear

Names that flow on back to yours
Numbers dialed months before
Frames of photos put away
Eternal bliss that wouldn't stay

Rain erasing sidewalk chalk
Reflections stay in where I walk
Puddles gather, yet can't forget
This very spot at first we met

Brian Dorn

## DARK IN ME

Welcome to my haunted house
Dare to see the dark in me
Suits of armor wait to joust
Eyes in portraits move to see

Stroke my ego, don't be shy
Give my id his equal pay
Watch the serpent slither by
My alter ego's chance to play

In the dungeon sleeps the creature
Securely cuffed in mounted chains
Disregard his ragged features
Please excuse the carpet stains

Behind the bookcase hides my secrets
Discretion swept up under rugs
The dark in me you haven't met
Struggles loose in warring tugs

Tempting me in carnal pleasure
Rewarding me if I dare
Accolades in grand measure
Disposing me in deep despair

Brian Dorn

## TEARS IN MY EYES

As you read my poems, might you think of me
If you find I'm lost, just leave me be
I'm not yours to save, only yours to please
Everything I write reveals our secrecy

Tangled in webs of truth or dare
Dangling from emotional snares
Publicly outing my private insides
Spilling my guts, my tongue untied
Anguishing over my every word
No sacred tenet left undisturbed

Sooner or later, I knew you'd realize
How our past events all seem to apply
Based in truth, discarded as lies
Each thinly veiled attempt to disguise

By now you must know what my words imply
All so obvious from the tears in my eyes
Soaked in emotion from which they cry
Strained from holding these feelings inside

Brian Dorn

## SUBLIMELY CONNECTING

My eyes seek to find yours
My hands reach to hold yours
My mouth craves to meet yours
My heart beats to be yours

Eyes lock and arms extend
Inhibitions blocked as elbows bend
Leaning closer with heads angled
Torsos embrace as necks are tangled
Bodies joining heart-to-heart
Souls mate as longing parts

Perfectly fitted as if by design
Your five fingers woven in mine
Coupled palms sublimely connecting
Severed love lines now intersecting
Sharing laughs and spending time
Captive souls forever entwined

"X" plus "Y" equates to you and me
The perfect math algebraically
The sum of which, to be exact
Is proof our values do attract

Brian Dorn

## STOP AND THINK

How great a man would I make
To love my foe for Jesus' sake

Who are you to cast these stones
As if your transgressions were unknown

So, this is what my speck has triggered
Your plank has left you so disfigured

What do you gain by judging me
Just whose reflection do you see

How great a man would I make
To love my foe for Jesus' sake
And, what's it prove to turn my cheek
A stronger man or a man turned weak

For if I might endow the power
To spare the world its final hour
Would I fend for just my brother
Or give myself to serve all others

How great a man would I make
To love my foe for Jesus' sake

Instilling fear, that's all you know
So much hate inside your soul
Our peace of mind, you wish to take
To punish us for our mistakes

Stop and think of what you've done
In whose name you load these guns
The fate of man now insecure
How great the cost of holy war

How great a man would I make
To love my foe for Jesus' sake

There is room for us all
No shortage of space
Rooms with no walls
Room for each race

There is plenty of room
Enough to go around
All of it reserved
For those Heaven bound

Brian Dorn

## ANOTHER STEP FORWARD

Seems by nature, we follow blind
Lost in this destructive grind

Our collective conscience, yet to find
Costing man his peace of mind

Another step forward, yet further behind
What to make of humankind

Man keeps thinking
He's got all the answers
While riddling the earth
With all types of cancers

Non-degradable plastics
And industrial waste
Our toxic emissions
Are a human disgrace

We've unbalanced the oceans
And upended the weather
Meteorologically speaking
We're bound to get wetter

Destroying the world
With our superior knowledge
It's time that our intellects
Go back to college

Brian Dorn

## PROFOUNDLY ATTRACTIVE

My eye you've caught
My line is taut
And I'm taking a good long look

My heart surely knows
It's arched like a bow
And my target is in sight

My mind is narrow
Straight as an arrow
And focused point-blank on you

Never before seen a smile so sheen
Never before ever lived out a dream
Never before adored anything more
Never before have I been more sure

I can't even begin to count
Nor quantify the immense amount
Of joy your smile brings

I can't even begin to show
Nor demonstrate the mirth bestowed
Solely from its presence

I can't find the words to write
Nor locate anything in sight
That's equivalent to it

You are profoundly attractive
As engaging as can be
Not merely on the surface
But deep down underneath

Brian Dorn

## HARD TO SAY

We've been over this before
How you're in need of something more
Needing to know I'm strictly yours
And intent on being sure
Yours to stable and yours to harness
Nothing more and nothing less

Nothing stays the way it should
All my love had somehow died
You held on for all you could
So honorable of you to try

Wish there was an easier way
Wrong of me to not reply
Who's at fault, it's hard to say
Wish I could have said good-bye

I'm not sure where you've been
But, you're always welcome back
Doesn't matter who said what when
My cruel statements, I retract

Brian Dorn

## TELEGRAM

I've made my presence felt
And gave it a good try
All of which I undermined
Before I'd even realized

I wish I could take back
Every faulty word I've pasted
If only I could backtrack
And recover what's been wasted

I should have been smarter
And made better choices
Attempted to barter
And adhered to the voices

I should have held back
And played it a little safer
Given you a bit more slack
And used up more eraser

I long to feel you in my arms
Exactly where it all began
Preceding my half-witted charms
Prior to my telegram

Brian Dorn

## UNDER AND OVER

Lying in grass searching under and over
Dying to find but one four-leaf clover
Never my fortune to find one before
Try as I might, I falter once more

If ever I were to find just one
I'd offer it to my prodigal son
Duly reward the maturing he's done
How lucky to know the man he's become

Life gives and it takes
A mix of joy and heartache
Good fortune and bad breaks
Celebrations and earthquakes

Things don't always happen
The way we think they should
Bad things often happen
But for the greater good

It's difficult to understand
The confounded nature of His plan
Things that we can't comprehend
That's the dilemma of mere man

Brian Dorn

## MY QUEEN

My pawns remain at the head of the line
Ready for battle, one square at a time
My queen and I stand side by side
From atop my rook we hide

But our battlefield has gotten dusty
My opponents' skills have grown rusty
We stand ready up on this shelf
Left to fend all by ourselves

My bishops wait in loyalty
Patiently devising a strategy
Waiting for our chance at war
To occupy this board once more

But electronics are now the way to go
Games with graphics and video
They say my knights move way too slow
Now just relics displayed for show

Brian Dorn

## OUT OF THE SHADOWS

I'm on the open road
Putting everything on hold
While I figure out where I'm going

I'm in route to somewhere
In time I know I'll be there
But it's taking longer than I'd hoped

Where to, I have no clue
I'd tell you if I knew
But I'll know it when I get there

I tend to give up too easily
I'm going to stick it out this time
Begin to roll with the punches
And conquer life's inclines

I've got to see this through
From the beginning to the end
I'm refusing to break
Or even to bend

I've made up my mind
And I'm unwilling to give in
I've never been more determined
And I'm playing to win

I've got to do it for me
And nobody else
I'm stepping out of the shadows
No longer doubting myself

There is no turning back
I'm in too deep already
This time, I'm playing for keeps
And I'm keeping rock steady

Brian Dorn

## TAKING AIM

Painting portraits with your words
Every expression of which I've heard
Adding letters with each careful stroke
Creating art through which you've spoke

Loading words with reckless abandon
Firing poems from a loose cannon
Taking aim at my soul companion
With every assault, you're still standing

Your feelings for me remain the same
Withstanding every hurtful rhyme
Doesn't matter who's to blame
Or, why we've crashed so many times

Wrong of me to punish you
With poetry and platitudes
Pent-up anger jotted down
Verbalized and paper bound

Spewing vengeance line by line
Planting barbs in clever rhymes
Time to let my pencil rest
And finalize my manifest

Brian Dorn

## FREEDOM'S NAME

Oh, sweet land of liberty
At least that's what you claimed to be
So, this is what freedom really means
To all but those from overseas

Auctioned off as your possession
By law, no need for compensation
Through it all, where was the shame
Owning man in freedom's name

Robbing them of self-respect
Grant no power to elect
Steal away their dignity
Compromising man's civility

Oh, sweet land of liberty
Still so hard to believe
Seems like only yesterday
How could it ever be that way

Brian Dorn

## PITFALLS

Waiting for his luck to change
Losing everything but his name
Strolling slots which never end
So many chances, zero to spend

Every pocket has run dry
Should have given lotto a try
Just a dollar and a dream
Not so simple as it seems

Maybe someone we once knew
Could be me, could be you

You've got no right to use that tone
Yelling at me on my telephone
Insisting that I pay my bills
Your voice emitting such a shrill

Why on earth do you do this work
You'd have to be crazy, or even berserk
Ruining lives with your harassing calls
Burying me in my own pitfalls

Doesn't your conscience bother you
Causing families to come unglued
Yours is the greater of our crimes
Selling your soul for the dollar sign

Continue your ungodly ways
You're bound to get your pay someday
In time, they'll collect on you
When the devil decides you're overdue

Maybe someone we once knew
Could be me, could be you

Lying on concrete, cup in hand
Vying attention where you stand
Wild hair and weathered face
Imagine living in his place

Dollar to spare, won't give it up
Too repulsed to feed his cup
Turn your head and walk away
Ignore his plight, leave no pay

Made his bed, there he lies
Amongst the garbage and the flies
Maybe someone we once knew
Could be me, could be you

Brian Dorn

## LONG PAST DUE

Being charged by you know who
Accusing me of loving you
A charge of which there's no defense
Considering the preponderance of evidence

She's digging deep for my confession
Accusing me of my obsession
Insisting the subject be addressed
My denials spark protest

No more need for arguments
All excuses have been spent
My innocence, I must attest
I say just let the matter rest

Passed it off as meaningless
My testimony, she rejects
In truth, there's grounds to be upset
My lack of forwardness, I so regret

If I were to whisper in your ear
All eight letters you've longed to hear
Would they spell three words to you
Or, might you reject them as long past due

Brian Dorn

## UNGLUED

Lately, I can't help but dwell
(Recollecting your show and tell)
On how things used to be
Way before my rhyming spree

Just when I'm sure I'm over you
Everything becomes unglued
All my thoughts of you return
Your embers re-ignite my burn

It keeps recurring randomly
How everything comes back to me
Just as I think the feeling's gone
It reemerges twice as strong

I try not to even think of you
But this strategy just doesn't do
I end up longing even more
It's not a cost-effective cure

I need to get these thoughts to stop
Try to get your gauge to drop
Tune down the ballyhoo
And steer my mind clear of you

Brian Dorn

## HIDDEN IN NIGHT

Poems recorded in black and white
Darkest reflections hidden in night
Written in mystery, revealed in plain sight
Intimate moments exposed in broad light

Close my eyes and lay away
Through darkened sights of silent days
Bonds wrapped loose, unraveling free
Awake to see what sleeps in me

Hidden desires, in life suppressed
Unburied in night, my dreams confessed
Spilling my soul of lusting changes
Visions of you, my subconscious arranges

Forced open and free - these feelings repressed
Piecing a puzzle love has undressed
Treasuring moments imagined with you
Wishing it be an illusion found true

Awake in unrest, my answer I find
All just a dream conceived out of mind
Fists pounding open the wall of my heart
Emotions emerge as fantasy parts

Closing my eyes, yet laying awake
Desperate to find what dreams I may make
Closing my eyes, yet laying awake
Desperate to find what dreams I may make

Brian Dorn

## I NEED A SIGN

Losing sight of wholesome faces
Forcing policy in foreign places
Memories linger of better days
Praying things won't stay this way

Opinions differ on every subject
Many agree and others object
What is right, who's to say
Praying things don't stay this way

Different voice but same old song
Know it's right but preach it's wrong
Just like games the children play
Praying things can't stay this way

Building bigger armories
Never finding harmony
Common sense gone astray
Praying people change their ways

Positions have been set in stone
Convictions sung in monotone
Views as hard as sculpted clay
The golden rule just tossed away

Please, my Lord, I need a sign
Lift my spirits and ease my mind
Anything Lord, just make it clear
Lead me away from all this despair

Please, my Lord, grant me a miracle
Teach me some kind of modern-day parable
Something remarkable, a marvelous sign
Something all-knowing, something divine

Brian Dorn

## INSIDE OF YOU

I sit and wait the eleventh hour
As love awaits for me
The clock spins slow tonight
Its hands to send me free

I think of embracing you
Making love this midnight hour
All of me inside of you
Warm in your mystic flower

Cursing the clock each second more
Finally the sign reads eleven
Soul on the gas, heart at the wheel
Driving the highway to heaven

Sexily dressed in sultry lace
Rose me in your crystal vase
Doped by shots of London gin
Play me like your mandolin

Digging treasure beneath the sheets
Hidden pleasures buried deep
By this map, "G" marks the spot
Trace the rainbow to the pot

Shovel in and shovel out
Lucky charms in spastic spouts
Sounds of muffled revelry
Fortunes in sweet ecstasy

I'd give in to all you say
To breathe you in and float away
Beyond the stars and galaxy
Together, universally

Brian Dorn

## DAZED AND UNSURE

Weighted down by all my stuff
Never feeling worthy enough

Overwhelmed by what I'm facing
All my thoughts perpetually racing

Feeling more and more rundown
Wearily burning to the ground

Praying for some peace of mind
Hoping that's what I'll find

Simply trying to measure up
But slipping further out of touch

Fifty years-old
My future's all but secure
The last thirty years
Have left me dazed and unsure

How will I know
When it's my turn to be up
Forever been waiting
For a streak of good luck

Age is catching up with me
My wrinkles all so plain to see
Time's no longer on my sIde
Wish I had just one more ride

Just to do it all again
I'd resolve to be a better man
Too bad you only get one chance
As it all becomes a passing glance

I'll make the best of what is left
To edify my final breath
Make amends for my mistakes
Right my wrongs for Heaven's sake

Brian Dorn

## TOPSY-TURVY

My two colleagues crossing borders
Sending courtship out of order
Relationships turned topsy-turvy
Loyalty is hardly worthy

Two worlds which don't belong
Melodies that sound all wrong
Nights filled with broken dreams
Harmony has turned to screams

Now you've seen the worst in me
The moment you brought up his name
Exposing me to jealousy
Defeating me in hurting games

How could you be seeing him
Left me feeling so betrayed
All my light, now gone dim
Insecure and so afraid

Every day becoming sadder
Trying not to think at all
All my confidence now shattered
How much farther will I fall

Look at what you've done to me
Reducing me to tatters
My lesson learned, I've come to see
That nothing really matters

Brian Dorn

## WHATEVER WILL BE

Rain is on its way
Regardless of what they say
They can't all be sunny days
Rain is on its way

Heavy, soaking rain
Days drenched in pain
Pouring harder every day
Washing dreams away

But, the sun is on its way
Regardless of what they say
They can't all be rainy days
The sun is on its way

Sometimes you have to give in
Just bare it and grin
And move on with your life

Difficulties come and go
There are bumps in the road
And plenty of twists and turns

Whatever will be - will be
Life is full of uncertainty
So expect the unexpected

The past is out of your hands
Beyond your scope of command
And outside your jurisdiction

So put yesterday aside
Hang on for the ride
And hope the best is yet to come

Just keep an open mind
Who knows what you might find
If you're willing to keep searching

Brian Dorn

## CHANGING WAYS

Trying to connect the dots
Giving it all I got
Up-front and on the spot
Writing my forget-me-nots

Her memory remains in me
Unwilling to leave me be
Relentlessly tugging to and fro
Stubbornly refusing to let me go

Leaves die brown as branches bend
Maples bare-boned by autumn's end
Early nights and shortened days
'Tis the time of changing ways

Felt her warmth chill to cold
What once was fresh, now grows old
I have no choice but to remember
This twentieth day of December

Love is a four-letter word
This I'd swear to any day
A word which we all have heard
But, one whose meaning fades away

Brian Dorn

## RUINED

The place that I was in
My tranquility within
The comfort I enjoyed
You've abruptly destroyed

My sworn love
Of which I was sure of
Certified and candid
You've carelessly disbanded

The very one I want
My trusty confidante
Of who I am so fond
You've severed that bond

The loyalty we spoke of
My confidential stuff
Of which I shared with you
You've flagrantly abused

The thing which I've adored
Everything I'd hoped for
All that love can bring
You've ruined everything

Brian Dorn

## WHAT'S THE USE

I'm a poet, not an architect
What you see isn't what you get
You've got to read between the lines

Every word spoken for
Concluding that less is more
Uncluttered and punctually barren

Writing it by ear
But are you hearing what I hear
I wonder if you're even listening

Fabricating my latest poem
One more to call my own
But I can't unearth the sound

Finding it difficult to rhyme
My creativity has flat-lined
And I'm at a loss for words

Feeling nickel and dimmed
I've lost days at a time
And my mind is lyrically spent

I'm down on my luck
Trying to regain my touch
But my pen will not cooperate

I'm in a bad way
It's getting worse every day
I'm in dire need of inspiration

I'm lollygagging in despair
Complaining art isn't fair
And contemplating quitting

What's the use in saying more
My words have all been heard before
Everything's been said and done
My battle fought, my peace begun
My pen has dueled with all its might
No more words left to write

Brian Dorn

## HER ATTRIBUTES

Her cursing is contagious
Her touch stimulating
Her stories outrageous
Her insults emasculating

Her anger adoring
Her imperfections attractive
Her nagging so boring
Her motions so active

She inspires me in my writing
Brings expression to my face
Her proposals are so inviting
Her presence makes my heart race

A heat that rises from her skin
Melts the ice I'm frozen in
So hot it burns me peach to red
Thawing streams within my head

She's my enduring protagonist
Whose attributes I do enlist
The incarnation of my poetry
The one I channel frequently

Brian Dorn

## IN GOD WE TRUST

Of all these faces I have seen
Millions of people, no two the same
Some so polite, others just mean
Many obscure, a few finding fame

Each of us living day to day
Finding ourselves among the masses
Numbered and labeled along the way
Divided into social classes

Some here today but gone tomorrow
A miracle to have ever been born
Searching for happiness, finding sorrow
Feeling beaten, tired and worn

Everyday meeting new strange faces
Wondering who they just might be
Each heading to different places
Isn't that what it means to be free

The faces of America
Including every one of us
Somehow diverting mass-hysteria
That's because In God We Trust

Brian Dorn

## WRITING POETRY

Writing poetry is hit and miss
Some poems come easy, others resist
Some get on board and others jump ship
Some gush out while others barely drip

Pen and paper don't always get along
One thinks they're right and the other is wrong
One is inspired while the other is bored
Each endlessly locked in a battle of words

Poetry is food for thought
Nourishing, but at a cost
Serving up my verbal best
Sometimes difficult to digest

Creating poetry from scratch
Trying to get the words to match
Emancipating my own say
Every idea boldly displayed

Every line subject to change
The syntax often rearranged
Erasing this and writing that
Scribbling like an acrobat

Setting my pride aside
Adjusting to life's turning tides
Journaling whatever comes
Invoking my artistic freedom

Writing poetry isn't easy
Every word must be in tune
Each stanza a symphony
Every lyric in bloom

Converting words into music
Each painstakingly chosen
Not everyone can hear it
But the silence is golden

We are figures of speech
Fending off writer's block
We're often offbeat
But the poetry rocks

Brian Dorn

## ALL WHICH WAY

You plant in me a rose
All which way it grows
Blooming from the start
Burning in my heart
Touching to my soul
Spreading through me whole
Spreading through me whole

Petals fall astray
Feelings wilt away
Left with jagged thorns
Tangled in and torn
Tearing us apart
Knife into my heart
Knife into my heart

Cutting stems to stout
Pruning branching doubts
Buds return to sprout
Roses blossom out
Returning me to you
Love begins anew
Love begins anew

Defending me from foes
In spite of what you hear

Shielding me from blows
In spite of what you see

Your devotion only grows
In spite of what I do

Don't ever let me go
Despite what you may know

You've got a chance to be with anyone
Every single person under the sun
To be with whoever you care to see
Why on earth would you choose me
Why on earth would you choose me

Brian Dorn

## STANDARD OF LIVING

Paying top-dollar for that Broadway show
Singing and dancing for all that dough
How about Barry in his Giants' cap
Making millions off the swing of a bat
So, that's what he's worth for playing a game
Shouldn't we all be paid just the same
I wonder how much a Fireman makes
Must be well paid for the courage it takes

I'm ashamed of our standard of living
Robbing those whom we should be giving
Draining the poor and fueling the rich
That's not my idea of legit politics

It's a swank new world as microwaves swirl
And satellites orbit the earth
The worldwide web, millions of minds being fed
As others are literally starving
It's a prosperous time as Wall Street climbs
And the needy are shamefully ignored

What's going on in the Third World
Who really cares if they live that way
Death, disease, and economic peril
Their kids are starving as ours play

Distended bellies and sunken eyes
It doesn't have to be that way
Hunger pains and desperate cries
If they only had the strength to play

Boys and girls desperate for help
Everyday more lives give way
Waiting for their nation to develop
Never getting the chance to play

The world's disparity is alarming
Some are hoarding while others are starving
The fat cats keep getting fatter
While the have-nots hardly matter
It's imperative that we share the wealth
Promote goodwill and economic health
We've got to stop behaving shortsighted
Begin to exist as humans united

We live in a world of hurt
Ignoring every sordid report
Every day is do or die
As we conveniently blind our eyes
It's going to take an empathetic attitude
A dramatic shift in social latitude
Everybody coming together
Each committed to making it better

Brian Dorn

## WISHING WELL

Peeking through darting eyes
Dodging as she hides her lies
Playing him and scheming me
Crumbling into what I see

Mercifully, she tells me so
Everything, just as I know
Breaking all within my skin
Soaking me in jealous sin

Consumed in her for so long
Left to part with only songs
Squeezed inside this vice of pain
Soiled, as my grace is stained

Needles buried through my flesh
So deep the hurt in every breath
Stones smash through glass sanity
Weakening in my immunity

In my thoughts is all I see
Dreaming she were here with me
Locked inside my cryptic cell
Drowning in her wishing well

Brian Dorn

## FOND MYSTERY

Every time my thoughts turn to you
Can't help but wonder if you think of me too
You crisscross my mind as I fumble about
Do you dial me in or do you tune me out

Contemplating which way to turn
Smother my feelings or let them burn
Measuring every uneven dimension
So in need of divine intervention

Perplexed by your duplicity
Suspended in fond mystery
Unsure of whether to inquire
So insecure in your desire

The hardest part is not knowing
Really unsure of what you're showing
Guessing whether to pursue or refrain
Neither rhyme nor reason still remain

Brian Dorn

## HIS GRACE

From crude nails, His body bleeds
"King of Jews" - the verdict reads
Along His brow, a piercing crown
As He suffers, skeptics frown

Wrought in pain, they mock His words
'Spencing justice with their swords
Beat Him down till barely living
But, by His grace, they've been forgiven

Two thousand years ago
Little did the world know
Of our Savior's merciful plan

Two thousand years ago
Little did the world know
That He'd be crucified by man

Two thousand years ago
Little did the world know
What we'd later come to understand

Christians are not perfect
Far from it, in fact
We all fall short of His glory
And need to circle back

We're all guilty as sin
And waver in our faith
We all need to givc thanks
For how He suffered in our place

We are too quick to judge
And too slow to forgive
We need to be more like Him
And love and let live

He settled our debt
As He conquered the cross
Proved that life is not over
And all is not lost

He demonstrated His love
As He suffered for us all
The least we can do
Is follow protocol

The last shall be first and first shall be last
The future is now and the blame has passed

It's like pressing rewind and beginning again
Erasing mistakes like they've never been

Changing course and rewriting history
It's being born again and living differently

Brian Dorn

## OVER THE LINE

I want my feelings back
You can't have them anymore
I'm afraid you will abandon them
Just as you've done before

Here I wander through my home
All alone, I write a poem
Helps to pass the time along
Makes me ponder what went wrong

No longer seeing him from you
Finding doubt in who I knew
It's clear your love's no longer true
Seems there's nothing I can do

You find me strange
Call me deranged
And tell me I'm in need of help

That I'm in decline
I've crossed over the line
And you have no empathy left

But if you know me so well
Than why can't you tell
That my poems are all about you

Brian Dorn

## THE ENDS OF THE EARTH

Humans are capable of horrific things
How could this ever be happening
Isn't it clear, enough is enough
We've got some nasty shit to clean up

How on Earth did we create such a mess
Leading the world into global distress
Is it still possible to reverse our course
Or, should we be bracing for even worse

What's the need for so much stuff
Haven't we already got enough
Still, we keep producing more
Most of which we've seen before
Another gadget, another spiel
Different spin but same old wheel

Advancing to the ends of the Earth
In our pursuit of moving forth
How much longer can we maintain this pace
We're rapidly running short on space

Brian Dorn

## POETRY IS SEXY

Poetry is sexy - Its lyrics aim to please
Poetry is sexy - Engaging in its tease

Poetry is sexy - It radiates with verb
Poetry is sexy - Every idyllic word

Poetry is sexy - Refined for purity
Poetry is sexy - Stripped of subtlety

Poetry is sexy - When read between the lines
Poetry is sexy - Laced with frilly rhymes

Poetry is sexy - Both singular and plural
Poetry is sexy - Every exclamatory swirl

Poetry is sexy - Grammatically raw
Poetry is sexy - Even typos and all

Poetry is sexy - Consummated publicly
Poetry is sexy - When performed properly

Poetry is sexy - Irrespective of its font
Poetry is sexy - Fashioned any way you want

Brian Dorn

## WAIT FOR ME

Would you wait for me
If I asked you to
Waited till I'm free
Free to be with you

Free to let you in
Free to hold your hand
Free to try again
And free to set a plan

Would you wait for me
To be face-to-face
Waited till I'm free
Free to plead my case

Free to socialize
Free to reunite
To be eye-to-eye
Free to make it right

So, will you wait for me
Fulfill my yearning need
Wait until I'm free
And connect with me

Brian Dorn

## MY EXCLUSIVE MUSE

The logistics of love, two souls forming one
Like a glove on a hand or the patty to a bun
It's not unusual in how the numbers add up
It's simple arithmetic like coffee to a cup
It's a natural reaction, quite easily done
The law of attraction, how two becomes one

You are my preferred brand name
The others are generically lame
To all of them, I bid adieu
My brand loyalty remains with you

You are my breath of fresh air
My day free of care
My cool summer breeze
And my converse disease

You are my refreshing malt
My first reflective thought
My recurring daydream
And my idea of serene

You are my finishing touch
My purely intuitive hunch
My sight for sore eyes
And my pleasant surprise

You are my guiding light
My perpetual delight
My contagious laugh
And my mutual half

You are my exclusive muse
My report of good news
The one I lobby for
Of whom I gladly implore

You are my plush amenity
My luxurious accommodation
My distraction from the world
My unequivocal elation

There is nothing more beautiful
No person, place or thing
Nothing that compares to you
You're my superlative plaything

No gem, no work of art
No earthly scenery
You are my staunch perennial
The basis for my jubilee

Brian Dorn

## AGITATED

You're overaggressive and overeager
In everything you choose to do
I'm over my head and beleaguered
And I'm agitated over you

I've been overlooked and overruled
Passed over and toppled too
You're a quick study and I've been schooled
And I'm agitated over you

You're overbearing and overly dramatic
A prima donna through and through
Overzealous and overly combative
And I'm agitated over you

I've been plowed under and pushed over
I'm overdrawn and overdue
You're undeterred and undaunted
And I'm agitated over you

You are intelligent for sure
And I haven't got a clue
You've left me feeling insecure
And agitated over you

Brian Dorn

## THE ONE YOU ADORE

So, my friendly blue jay
What's this game you've come to play
Perched upon my fence post
You're the one I see the most

Posing, in hopes of gaining my attention
Oh, so aware of your feminine intentions
So patiently waiting day after day
Longing to fly me far, far away

When you're 50 and I'm sixty-four
Will I still be the one you adore

When you're 60 and I'm seventy-four
Will you still feel the same for sure

When you're 70 and I'm eighty-four
Will you grow weary of my folklore

When you're 80 and I'm ninety-four
Will you even want me around anymore

When you're 90 and I'm a hundred-and-four
Will you still be the one I adore

Brian Dorn

## YOUR FOOTSTEPS

Walking on water
Among other glorious things
Is exclusively licensed
To heavenly beings

The same can be said
For the creation of life
Man keeps infringing
On God's copyright

Beware of scholarly achievers
Professing to know what life's about
Making skeptics of believers
In the business of planting doubts

Peddling science in place of scripture
Asserting their polluted clout
Disregarding the spiritual picture
Leaving the essentials out

Teacher, You've taught us well
Your words are truly unparalleled
But, it's not easy to follow Your lead
The world incessantly intercedes

Distracting us from Your direction
Befuddled by life's intersections
Taking wrong turns and losing our way
Veering further from You each day

Every time I do stray
will You seek to find me

What if I am fooled to pray
to idols and false prophets

Though so often I may ask
will You still forgive me

How do I fulfill this task
that You lay before me

Maybe I'm not strong enough
to follow in Your footsteps

I'm afraid the sea's too rough
to be a fisherman

Brian Dorn

## GROWING UP

The ancestral tree takes root in me
Coated in red and yellow leaves
Nowhere to go, no yearning to move
Stoic it stands with nothing to prove

Growing up on Anna Lane
Raised embracing the mundane
Every day basically the same
Growing up on Anna Lane

Never any cause for change
A neighborhood neatly arranged
On the bus, off to school
Obeying every common rule

Growing up on Anna Lane
Little worthy of acclaim
Everything perfectly plain
Growing up on Anna Lane

Reach out to the leaves
As they fall from the trees
All at once the wind makes them run

They fly off alone
Each on their own
To wherever the breeze sends them

Now free to roam
Away from their home
Declaring their own independence

Brian Dorn

## AROUSING REFLECTION

Eyes reflecting ocean green
Impossible to be unseen
I gaze inside and swim within
Engulfed inside her whirlwind

She has neutralized my strength
And apprehended my emotions
Obstructed my wavelength
And commandeered my devotion

She boggles my mind
Never failing to impress
She's one of a kind
She's pure elegance

She embodies perfection
From her halo to her toes
Arousing reflection
With her magnanimous glow

The warmth of her smile
Penetrates to my soul
Her lips curl softly
As she whispers "hello"

My eyes duck to hide
The truth they won't show
In one bashful moment
I let it all go

Brian Dorn

## YOUR ESSENCE

It doesn't come easy
You have to try and try
Let your mind wander
Let your insights apply

Relentlessly digging
Deep down to your core
Into your abyss
Keep digging for more

Your deep dark secrets
Your buried black box
Those things you keep hidden
That place you keep locked

Assert your feelings
Disclose the unknown
Extract your essence
Reveal it in poems

It's yours to share if you dare
At anytime and anywhere
Summon it and it will come
Unleash your phenomenon

Remove the barricade from the door
Let your spirit freely soar
Just release your inner-source
Let your purpose run its course

The two of you in tandem
No longer living random
Capable of anything
Anything that life can bring

Brian Dorn

## SLEIGHT OF HAND

Sleight of hand, she waves her wand
Onto me her magic bonds
Casting spells with my emotions
Stirring passion in her potions

Lassoes me with roping flicks
Folds my hands with sly card tricks
Stacking decks with foolish jokers
Bluffing me in dirty poker

Searching words in puzzle mazes
Guessing letters in cryptic phrases
Solving clues across and down
Mixing jumbles with pronouns

All her statements contradicting
Making promises, seldom sticking
Nixing kisses with odd looks
All caught up in romance books

Cold as ice, yet sweet as wine
Faking sick but feeling fine
Duping me with pouty lips
Baiting me with Freudian slips

Strange how she can pull me in
Cheating me so she can win
Switching sides of my heart
Turning tides like Bonaparte

Always reason to battle wits
Sometimes prone to passive fits
Nothing ever simply stated
Everything all complicated

Brian Dorn

## CLUELESS

I've got reason to believe
He's only a formality
You're supposed to be with me
Not your current company

Playing by the rules
But being taken for a fool
How could I be so clueless

You crank my handle and up I pop
Playing me like a Jack-in-the-box
You shut the lid as you cram me in
Readying me to surface again

Playing by the rules
But being taken for a fool
How could I be so clueless

Scanning stations on the radio
Channels come and channels go
Losing one as another starts
Signaling another change of heart

Playing by the rules
But being taken for a fool
How could I be so clueless

You dragged me off my feet
Left me crumpled in a heap
And unable to recover my bearings

I'm in a state of desperation
Painfully aware of your relation
And uncertain of what to do next

Brian Dorn

## HIS HUMOR

It's his nature to be friendly
His kindness is so easily seen
But his imagination wanders
In his mind, he's fancy-free

He's open and he's candid
And his humor is unique
Offbeat by standard norms
But not hesitant to speak

In many ways, no different
But other ways bizarre
In need of understanding
He's not the way we are

In many ways, he's better
His sincerity, in fact
He's honest and he's forthright
There's no losing sight of that

Brian Dorn

## SAD POEMS

Sad poets tend to be misunderstood
As their poetry does as it should
Expressing woe, though doing it good
Just like any truly sad poet would

Sad poems are inherently pure
There's always a demand for more
Whether a classic or obscure
Sad poems are sound literature

Sad poems are my loyal friends
Helping my sad heart to mend
Resistant to passing trends
Surviving till the bitter end

This sad-poem frame of mind
Of which I've often been maligned
The forlorn, melancholic kind
The likes of which I am inclined

Whether plain sad or infinitely sadder
Every single sad poem matters
Each the product of a sad mind-state
Of which many (sadly) can relate

Brian Dorn

## THIS DAY

It's blessings and heartache
Harmony and strife
Long shots and lucky breaks
It's the assortment of life

It's sci-fi and old school
Sometimes the going gets rough
Expect both praise and ridicule
Life's an assortment of stuff

One, two, three, four
What's this day have in store
Five, six, seven, eight
You'll lose it if you hesitate
Nine, ten, eleven, twelve
Use it to improve yourself

Thirteen, fourteen, fifteen, sixteen
This is not the time to dream
Seventeen, eighteen, nineteen, twenty
Take this day and live it plenty
Twenty one, two, three, and four
What's tomorrow have in store

Every day, a river flows
In some way, a person grows
Every day's a picture show
What's to happen, no one knows
Cameras roll, our lives exposed
Everything passes, anything goes

Brian Dorn

## TAKING IT SLOW

You've been waffling all along
Unsure of whether we belong
Forever yours, but never mine
We're impossible to define

You're taking it slow
And enjoying the view
I've got nowhere to go
And I'm waiting on you

I'll keep on waiting
For as long as it takes
However frustrating
I'll languishly wait

Unable to penetrate the surface
Beneath your guarded exterior
Confined to cells of noble purpose
Locked within your interior

Everything I care to know
Valued beyond measure
The very jewels you won't bestow
Your strictly private pleasures

You're playing hard to get
Ignoring my attention
Earning my respect
By avoiding apprehension

You're keeping me in check
Foiling my intentions
Assessing what I'll try next
But too juvenile to mention

Brian Dorn

## ATTEMPTING FATE

Composing words of pleasing sounds
Purposeful and written down
Contributing my point of view
Custom made, by hand, for you

Encasing passion verse creates
With my pen attempting fate
In painful truths and novel fiction
Writing sentiments in vague diction

Clouded feelings darken me
Graying skies of reality
Contained emotions coursing free
Pouring rain of fantasy

Reciting dreams I've come to find
Deep within my tainted mind
Tangled in vines of secrecy
Choking us in its deceit

Composed in words of varied tones
Dispersed within redundant poems
Finding reference in my rhymes
Accusing me of subversive crimes

In every act I could imagine
Concealed within poetic pageant
Revealing thoughts in all their splendor
Upon their mercy, I surrender

Brian Dorn

## POLITICS

Republican or Democrat
Really, what's the choice in that
Doesn't say much for democracy
If they are all we ever see

What's the point of a closed debate
Watching two pawns reiterate
How about another point of view
Fifty heads are better than two

A candidate from every state
A pageant of potential magistrates
A ballot with legitimate options
An election worthy of our adoption

Republican or Democrat
Really, what's the choice in that

Chill out, the Cold War is over
Animosity has mutually sobered
Let's put an end to this fiasco
Isn't it time we talk with Castro

Extend our hand to our neighbor
They're likely to return the favor
This feud has labored long enough
Why must our policies be so tough

Might no longer makes it right
We're both within each other's sight
Let's welcome them with open arms
I doubt they'll do us any harm

Republican or Democrat
Really, what's the choice in that

We're off to see "The Wizard of Is"
Giving testimony in the form of a quiz
Can't determine if it's false or true
Oh, so ambiguous number forty-two
Wooing us with verbal gymnastics
Confusing me of what the fact is
Denying every partisan accusation
No wonder he's in charge of our nation
Such a deceptively dazzling dialog
Linguistically leaving us in his fog

Republican or Democrat
Really, what's the choice in that

Brian Dorn

## SHORT OF EXPECTATIONS

Penning a locket
Laid bare in your midst
A memento of us
As we cease to exist

We both thought this love would last
But it's so obvious our prime has passed
So, what's the point of even trying
It's finally time we stop denying

It is better that you know
That's my reason for telling you so
It's your call how this will end
Maybe enemies, maybe friends

All my past relations
Falling short of expectations
I've got only myself to blame

Considering what might have been
It's too bad they had to end
I'm my own worst enemy

Annulling my past escapades
Obsessing over yesterday
The future is my only hope

Writing from my heart
Desperate for a brand new start
Attempting to reassert myself

Beginning a new chapter
Steering clear of disaster
Weary of the same pitfalls

My abilities in doubt
Words scattered all about
Trying to make sense of it all

Brian Dorn

## PAIN AND POETRY

Dying is a fact of life
In fact, it's guaranteed
Each and every one of us
Are among a dying breed

Dying is a certainty
That much we all know
But the question still remains
As to when and where we'll go

Is death a new beginning
Or just the means to an end
In time we all will find
What awaits around the bend

I walk along Niagara's ledge
Moving closer to the edge
Is this where it's meant to end

If I were to step on in
Might it cleanse me of my sin
Or plunge me into total darkness

When the current takes me down
Will I fight, or peacefully drown
Deep beneath among the stones

Opening the floodgates
Letting emotions rush out
Nearly drowning in the process
But that's what poetry's about

Pain and poetry go hand in hand
Without one, the other is bland
Lancing the wound and letting it bleed
Fulfilling its cathartic need

Brian Dorn

## THESE THINGS

Writing in seclusion
Me and my illusions
Letting feelings roam
Confessing them in poems

Searching out my deepest thoughts
Examining my every fault
Letting all these things be known
As every poem becomes its own

I can't help but wonder
If you partake in my poems
Do you ever obsess
Over what I've made known

And what you might think
Of what I have written
Your private reaction
To my public admittance

Every poem of endearment
Spelling out my affections
My faulty presumptions
And biased perceptions

My meandering feelings
And internal reflections
My fabric transparent
And discarding discretion

Brian Dorn

CPSIA information can be obtained at www.ICGtesting.com
Printed in the USA
BVOW06s1244020316

438755BV00011B/259/P